cklace t-shirt studded stunner s
rt no-sweat scarf, top and jean
ace tank top ru W9-AWB-850 ress
ble heads jeweled necklace ch
elet ribbon watch set button bro
rammed velvet bangles ballerin
bag customized tote bag polka-
e-in conditioner healing hands
k shakers chocolate mint cooki
lotion cocoa butter bonbons s
erfume boys-of-the-week panti
ees tanks for everything! tie-dy
shirt chain t-shirt sequined tank
rk tank and skirt ribbon-front h
ded necklace key necklace bec
rated ballet flats painted straw
ppers grab bag ring handle bag
hakeup bag avocado mask for
honey & almond body scrub win
scrub peppermint bath salts e
e soaps fizzy bath bombs lip gl

COSMO *girl!*

Make it Yourself

50 **Fun** and **Funky** Projects

Hey CosmoGIRL!s,

You may not know it, but you're the most positive, can-do, proactive group of girls that has ever walked the earth. I know that may sound like a big statement, but it's true. You're smarter than ever, you're more independent, and no one can trick you because you see right through it. Plus, you know more about what you want out of life than I did when I was your age, or your mom did, or your grandma. You have a lot more to choose from, that's for sure. And you're excited to try anything and everything!

All of these things about you have come together to create this whole "do it yourself" thing that everyone (including your mom and grandma, probably!) is crazy about. Yes, you were the real trendsetters, even though most people may not stop to realize it. Before *Extreme Makeover: Home Edition* or *Trading Spaces* or any of those DIY shows existed, *CosmoGIRL!* was showing you how to redo your room and your wardrobe—your way. Because doing things yourself isn't just about having fun and saving money, it's about making it yours, and that's what you're all about. Tailoring your stuff to your unique personality. The fact is, you shop the same places your friends do, but that doesn't mean you want to all look and act exactly alike, right? Of course not! You've got to give it your own unique spin.

Contents

Design by Margaret Rubiano

Library of Congress Cataloging-in-Publication Data

CosmoGIRL! Make It Yourself / The editors of CosmoGIRL!.
    p. cm.
  Includes index.
  ISBN-13: 978-1-58816-624-1
  ISBN-10: 1-58816-624-4
  1. Clothing and dress. 2. Beauty, Personal.
  TT507.C665 2006
  746.9'2—dc22

                                2006017182

10 9 8 7 6 5 4 3 2 1

Published by Hearst Books
A Division of Sterling Publishing Co., Inc.
387 Park Avenue South, New York, NY 10016

CosmoGIRL! and Hearst Books are trademarks of Hearst Communications, Inc.

www.cosmoGIRL.com

For information about custom editions, special sales, premium and corporate purchases, please contact Sterling Special Sales Department at 800-805-5489 or specialsales@sterlingpub.com.

Distributed in Canada by Sterling Publishing
c/o Canadian Manda Group, 165 Dufferin Street
Toronto, Ontario, Canada M6K 3H6

Distributed in Australia by Capricorn Link (Australia) Pty. Ltd.
P.O. Box 704, Windsor, NSW 2756 Australia

Manufactured in China

Sterling ISBN 13: 978-158816-624-1
        ISBN 10: 1-58816-624-4

COSMOgirl!

Make it Yourself

50 Fun and Funky Projects

The Editors of
CosmoGIRL!

Hearst Books
A Division of Sterling
Publishing Co., Inc.
New York

And that's what all the projects in *Make It Yourself* are meant for . . . these are the best of the best DIY ideas for clothes, accessories, and even beauty products. So that everyone will ask, "Where did you get that? Can I get it?" And you can say, "You can't buy it because it's an original. But I can show you how you can create your own!" Making stuff yourself is just another way to prove how smart, positive, independent, proactive, open-minded and unique you are.

So have fun with these DIY's . . . and wear or use them like a badge of honor. Because the world needs to know how absolutely, positively unprecedented you are.

Love,

Susan

P.S. Send me your Do-It-Yourself ideas—I'd love to put them in a future issue of *CosmoGIRL!* Email me anytime at susan@cosmogirl.com.

why make it yourself?

Why not! On top of impressing your family and friends with your cleverness, creativity, and skill when you present them with unique, handmade, from-the-heart gifts, it's also a great way to copy the style of your fave celebs—and save a ton of money while you're at it. And who knows…if you get really good, you may even decide to start your own side business and turn a pastime into cash time!

This book is divided into three sections: Clothing, Accessories, and Beauty. Wherever you begin, note that all of the projects have a difficulty rating (easy, medium, hard), so you may want to try the simple ones first and work your way up.

basic techniques

Before you dive into becoming a master of Make It Yourself, here's what you need to know.

sewing

Already know how to sew? Great—you're well on your way to mastering many of these fun and fabulous projects! If not, don't worry. The projects that call for sewing only require simple stitching. Also, all the sewing can be done quickly by hand, so even if there's a sewing machine in the house, you won't have to break it out! Here are some basic tips for stitching that's "sew" easy:

- **Before trying to poke the end of your thread through the tiny eye of your needle, moisten the eye. The thread should slip right in. Really!**

- Always start with an 18-inch length of thread. Longer will just get tangled, but shorter might be too little—it's easy to cut off extra at the end and hard to make a knot when there's barely anything left to tie.
- Keep stitches small, tight, and close together.
- Make a double—or even triple—knot before cutting off excess thread.
- For seams and hems, try iron-on seam tape instead of sewing. It's quicker and easier!

other ways to "make it stick"

A hot-glue gun can be used for embellishing some fabric projects, but it's not ideal for making seams or gluing small items. Craft glue is better for small pieces or when you want something to be flexible. When you use a glue gun, spread out the glue while it is still hot with a popsicle stick or even a butter knife. Keep in mind that the faster you get the glue applied, the smoother it will turn out.

basic equipment

You don't need to buy fancy gear and supplies for our fashion or beauty projects. A few basics can go a long way. If you can't find them around the house, try a craft store or large discount store. Here are some things you should always have on hand:

- needles of different sizes and lots of different colors of thread
- a sharp pair of scissors
- seam ripper
- needle-nose pliers
- tweezers
- straight and safety pins
- hot-glue gun/glue sticks
- craft cement
- measuring tape/rulers
- basic cooking gear

where to find it

Many of the items you'll need to do these projects may already be in your house, like a plain t-shirt, an inexpensive watch, or even some of the foods used in the Beauty section (avocados, baking soda). Others you'll have to buy specially. You can check the Internet for deals, but if you're the type of girl who'd rather check-out the merchandise first, here's where to look:

craft store

A craft store is easily one of the best places to find supplies because you'll be able to find just about everything there—stuff is usually organized by type of craft, so think if the thing you're look-ing for is used for sewing, embellishment, scrapbooking, or what:

- **fabric**
- **fabric paint**
- **mini-airbrush tool**
- **fabric stickers**
- **hot-glue gun and glue sticks**
- **glitter glue pen**
- **craft glue**
- **ribbons**
- **charms**
- **rhinestones**
- **pom-poms**
- **sequins**
- **buttons**
- **tassels**
- **silver chain**
- **beads**
- **bead sorter boxes**
- **grated beeswax**
- **Velcro**

large discount stores

A store stocked with bargains may be your best bet for getting your hands on these products:

- **soap or candy molds**
- **spice canisters**
- **foil candy wrappers**
- **bead sorter boxes**
- **decorative shoelaces**
- **plastic tablecloth**

health food store

These stores sell natural and organic foods. You can find one in almost any town. Products to use with this book that can be found there include:

- **organic ingredients**
- **essential oils (fragrant concentrated plant extracts)**
- **aloe vera gel**
- **shea butter**
- **turbinado sugar (a.k.a. "sugar in the raw")**

grocery store

Depending on the size of your supermarket chain, you can find almost everything you need in life at a grocery store. For the projects in this book, keep an eye out for:

- **Epsom salts (different than regular salt/check the health section)**
- **sea salt**
- **food coloring**
- **glycerine soap**

Now get ready, get set—make it yourself!

easy

medium

hard

clothing

Making your own wardrobe, or at least pieces of it, means **you won't have to worry** about showing up at a party wearing the same outfit as someone else. That's enough of a reason, but there are lots of others. For example, how many stores do you know that sell truly, **one-of-a-kind clothing?** And think about how much you'd have to spend for a seven-day assortment of **cleverly decorated** white tank tops—considering each one could run you about $25 in stores? Try out the styles in tanks for everything! on page 40 and **spend only a fraction** of that! Then there's the celeb thing. How many times have you gone wild over a top or dress that **your style icon** was wearing, and when you looked at how much she spent on it, you freaked out? Well, take a deep breath! In this section, you'll learn how to copy some of these **cool and original pieces,** like a form-fitting ruched tube dress on page 16 and a really cute chain t-shirt on page 34, without going broke. Once you **master the art** of handcrafted couture, you may never go back to retail!

tie-dyed **miniskirt**

Spill some tea on a pair of your chinos, and you'll end up with a cool skirt. How'd that happen?!

medium

- 1 pair light-colored pants
- 8 teabags of black tea
- scissors and seam ripper
- rubber bands

1. Cut the legs off the pants 6 inches below the crotch.

2. Use a seam ripper to open up the seams on the inside of the legs and along the curved part of the crotch.

3. Slip the skirt over your ironing board and overlap the crotch points on the front so they lie flat. Iron them and then sew the layers together. Do the same on the back. Twist the skirt tightly and secure with rubber bands.

4. Boil 3 quarts of water in a large pot. Add the teabags. Let the teabags steep for about 10 minutes. Dip the skirt in, let it get completely saturated, and take it out.

5. Remove the rubber bands. Untwist the skirt and let it dry to set the color. Then rinse and hang to dry. Iron, and it's ready to wear!

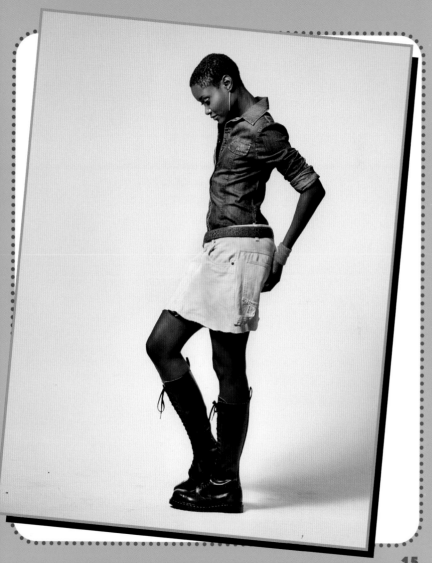

ruched tube dress

Here's a perfect outfit for spending a night on the town with friends!

- **1 yard of pink knit fabric**
- **3 yards $^3/_8$-inch-wide elastic**
- **measuring tape**
- **scissors and pins**
- **needle and pink thread**

1. Measure the fullest part of your bust. Add 16 inches to that number. Lay your fabric flat and cut it to be as wide as this sum—make sure you use the stretchiest direction of the knit as the width.

2. Fold fabric in half lengthwise (right side in) and stitch the 36-inch edges together to form a tube.

3. Cut 3 pieces of elastic, each the size of your bust measurement. Sew ends of each one together to form 3 elastic rings.

4. Fold down one end of fabric tube ½ inch. Place one elastic ring around the tube on top of the folded over fabric. Stretch the elastic to fit the fabric and pin in a few places. Then stitch the elastic to the fabric, pulling taut as you go.

5. Slip another ring around the tube, 3 inches below the first one. Stitch. Repeat 3 more inches down with the third elastic ring.

6. Put the tube on. Decide how long your dress should be. Take it off and cut off most of the extra fabric. Hem the bottom. Turn right side out. Now slip it on—off you go!

boys-of-the-week
panties

Just follow these easy instructions to make a personalized set to last a whole week! What a funny present for a friend who has everything.

- **7 pairs of plain cotton panties**
- **tube of silver metallic fabric paint**
- **14 pieces of $\frac{1}{8}$-inch-wide 20-inch-long satin ribbons in 7 different colors**
- **7 charms**
- **silky scarf (optional)**
- **seam ripper**
- **needle and thread**

1. Pick seven guys' names. Choose an M name for Monday (Mike), a T name for Tuesday (Tom), etc. Write one name in silver fabric paint across the front center of each pair of panties. Let dry 2 hours.

2. With seam ripper, poke 4 tiny holes on front left side of panties, $\frac{1}{2}$ inch in from seam. Make all of the holes $\frac{1}{2}$ inch apart. Repeat on right side.

3. Turn panties over. Repeat holes on the back left side and back right side so they line up with front holes.

4. Starting with the left side, thread a piece of ribbon through all 8 holes to form little Xs (like lacing a shoe). Tie a knot to secure. Cut off excess. Then repeat on right side.

5. Stitch a charm onto the back of the panty at the center top (like on ours, see below).

6. Make 6 more pairs and wrap all 7 in a silky scarf, if desired, as a gift.

patchwork
tank and skirt

See how you can turn what was old into . . . gold. Mission impossible? We think not!

- t-shirt
- iron-on seam tape
- bandanna
- pair of old jeans
- old sweatshirt
- scissors
- seam ripper
- needle and thread

tank

1. Cut a V into the neck of the t-shirt and then cut off the sleeves. Cut the bandanna into four 2-inch-wide strips.

2. Use iron-on seam tape, following instructions on package, to attach strips to the tank in a Union Jack pattern (as in the picture at right): Place 2 strips in a cross shape with the center at the middle of the shirt. Use the last 2 strips in a wide X-shape.

skirt

1. Cut the legs off the jeans about 6 inches below the crotch.

2. Use a seam ripper to open up the seams on the inside of the legs and along the curved part of the crotch.

3. Slip the skirt over your ironing board and overlap the crotch points on the front so they lie flat. Iron them and then sew the layers together. Do the same on the back.

4. Cut out any quirky decal from an old sweatshirt. Stitch around it (or use iron-on tape) to attach it to the skirt.

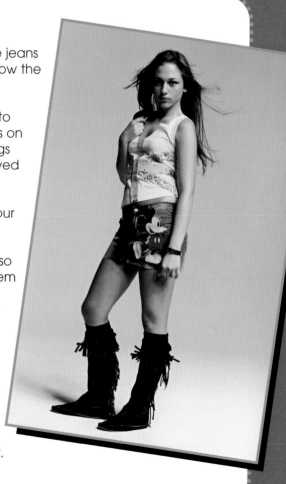

no sweat scarf, top, and jeans

Recycle an old outfit into something completely unique, just like you!

- old sweater
- old elastic-waist skirt (not too short)
- pair of full-length white jeans
- seam ripper
- scissors
- needle and thread
- black permanent marker

scarf

Cut sleeves off the sweater and save the sweater to wear when it's not too cold. Use seam ripper to open the sleeve seams. Cut off curved top of each sleeve—trash or save. Sew the sleeves together along the newly cut edges.

top

Wear the skirt as a billowy tube top. If hem falls below your hips, it's too long—cut the off the bottom.

jeans

Cut the jeans into capris. With a black permanent marker, draw (or stencil) designs on the right thigh.

jeweled necklace
t-shirt

Colored gemstones and ribbon turn a boring shirt into an exciting way to show off your personal style!

easy

- **1 plain long-sleeved crewneck t-shirt**
- **1 yard of 1-inch-wide ribbon**
- **assorted imitation gemstones**
- **hot-glue gun and glue sticks**
- **scissors**

1. Starting 3 inches down from the tee's shoulder seams, lay out gemstones in a "necklace" shape. When you're happy with how it looks, carefully hot-glue them down.

2. Cut ribbon in half. Turn edge of one end under ½ inch and hot-glue it down to form hem. Hot-glue hemmed end of ribbon directly above rhinestones on one side. Repeat with other piece of ribbon on the other side. Tie the ribbons at the back of your neck in a bow.

cutout **t-shirt**

Turn a simple t-shirt and end-of-their-life-span tights into a unique fashion statement!

- **old tights**
- **fitted short-sleeved t-shirt**
- **scissors**
- **needle and thread that matches t-shirt**

1. Cut off the legs of your old tights below the crotch, then snip the feet off at an angle. The 2 nylon legs will become sleeves on your new shirt.

2. Stitch the thigh part of one leg inside the sleeve of the t-shirt about 1 inch above the bottom edge (see picture). Repeat with the other leg and sleeve.

3. Draw a small heart (about the size of a golf ball) onto the t-shirt, next to the shoulder, then carefully cut it out.

4. Decide how much you'll charge when people ask you to (please, pretty please!) make them a shirt like yours.

studded **stunner**

Sparkly sleeves on a plain top (we used a black thermal) add some bling to any outfit!

- **long-sleeved cotton knit top**
- **gold and silver studs with prongs, 2 or more styles, enough to form cuffs on your garment**
- **white chalk fabric marker**
- **small needle-nose pliers**

1. Arrange the studs to form cuffs on your garment in a pattern you like. We used two styles of studs and arranged them in rows, varying the size and spacing.

2. One at a time, lift each stud slightly, make a chalk mark under it, and then set it aside. To keep track of your pattern as you remove the studs, lay them on your table in the same sequence.

3. Now place one stud over a chalk mark and push the prongs through the shirt so they poke out on the inside.

4. Use the pliers to bend the prongs against the fabric.

5. Repeat steps 3 and 4 to attach the rest of the studs. Sweet!

special-tees

Make cupid proud by turning a white t-shirt into a Valentine tribute.

word games ▶

Use a mini-airbrush tool or fabric markers to cover a white t-shirt with your favorite phrase or words in diagonal rows. Cut off the sleeves to make a tank. Then cut a 1-inch strip of fabric from a sleeve to make a bow and sew to the front at the neckline.

crowning glory ▶

Cut out words and photo images
from an old white t-shirt. Use colored
thread to stitch them onto a new
shirt in a different pattern.

◀ love spell

Use a glitter glue pen to write
your favorite Valentine's Day
word on a white t-shirt. Hot-glue
on some imitation gemstones for
even more sparkle.

heart candy ▲

Cut out hearts from solid fabric and
sew them onto a white t-shirt with ¾-length sleeves. Then
safety-pin funky buttons, bows, and charms all over.

boys 'n' arrows ▶

With thin fabric markers draw your own cartoon character and arrow hearts on a white t-shirt. Cut the sleeves off to make a tank. Finish with a funny sentence about boys or love.

◀ face time

Take a cool stencil (try a face or hearts) and fabric-paint it on a white long-sleeved t-shirt. Sew on a yarn pom-pom from the craft store at one shoulder for added color and detail.

chain **t-shirt**

**Transform a plain black t-shirt into a unique top
with open sides and attitude to match!**

medium

- **1 black cotton crewneck
  t-shirt**
- **4 ¹/₈ yards of thin silver chain**
- **scissors**
- **needle and black heavy-duty
  thread**
- **white chalk**
- **ruler**
- **2 safety pins**

1. Cut off the neck binding and both sleeves of the t-shirt.

2. Measure ½ inch below one armhole, and mark with
   chalk on side seam. From this mark, measure and mark
   horizontally 2 inches toward the front of the shirt and
   2 inches toward the back of the shirt (4 inches total).

3. Measure 1 inch above the bottom hem of the shirt,
   and mark with chalk on side seam. From this mark,
   again, measure and mark horizontally 2 inches on
   each side of the seam.

4. Connect the top and bottom markings with vertical lines to form a long narrow rectangle. Cut out the rectangle so the entire side of the shirt is now open, like a window. Repeat at the other side seam.

5. Pin one end of chain to one shoulder of shirt; then drape chain across to other shoulder and pin. Repeat back and forth, draping and pinning. Leave one length of chain to dangle. Thread the needle and knot the thread ends together so you can sew with two strands. Sew the chain to the shirt where pinned; remove pins.

sequined **tank top**

The options are endless for making simple tanks into works of art. This sparkly version is great for colored tops or any LWT (little white tank).

medium

- 1 plain cotton tank top
- 2 yards of 1-inch-wide elastic sequin trim
- tape measure
- scissors
- straight pins
- needle and thread

1. Put the tank top on. Measure completely around one armhole. Cut 2 pieces of sequin trim this long plus 1 inch.

2. Now measure completely around the neckline. Cut a piece of sequin trim this long plus 1 inch.

3. Take off the tank top. Pin the trim loosely around the armholes—start and end at each underarm seam.

4. To hand sew trim onto tank, take a few stitches in one place, knot and cut the thread, and then stitch again about 1 inch away. Repeat around each armhole. This will let the trim and the tank stretch with you.

5. Pin and stitch the trim around the neckline in the same way, starting and stopping—neatly!—in the back.

shoelace tank top

Fun shoelaces help personalize a plain tank.

medium

- 1 white ribbed tank top
- 1 pair decorative shoelaces, at least 20 inches long
- scissors
- 1 charm, stud, or a few imitation rhinestones (optional)
- needle and thread
- ruler

1. Cut the back of the tank to match the scoop in the front. Fold under the cut edge and sew it down.

2. Lay the tank flat. Measure and mark 4 inches down from top seam (or fold) of each shoulder strap in both front and back, then cut off the straps.

3. Snip off plastic ends of laces. Cut two 20-inch-long pieces of shoelace to be used as straps.

4. Place one shoe lace flat on a table. Bring the two ends together so the bottom of lace forms a U.

5. Place the very center of this U on the cut edge of one front tank strap. Stitch it down along the cut edge of the strap.

6. Bring the two ends straight back (forming a double strap) and stitch them to the outer edges of the cut strap on the back.

7. Repeat on the opposite side of the tank with the other shoe lace to make the second strap.

8. For extra detail, stitch a little charm, attach a stud, or spell out your friend's initial in rhinestones right below the right strap.

tanks for everything!

With a white tank top and a hot-glue gun, you can create a masterpiece faster than you can say Picasso!

shimmer down, now! ▶

Hot-glue large paillettes (flat sequins with a hole in the top instead of the center) in horizontal rows, overlapping each paillette until front of straps and top third of tank top are covered.

◀ brass act

Hot-glue ruffled gingham trim to bottom, a gingham bow to center of neckline, and 2 brass buttons below the bow.

wood you? ▶

Lay out a variety of wooden
beads in a pattern you like
along the straps and top front
of the tank top. Then hot-glue
the beads down.

◀ juicy fruits

Hot-glue 2-inch-wide scalloped
crochet trim around neckline.
Hot-glue crocheted fruit as
accents to center of collar
and bottom of tank top.

bowed over ▶

Hot-glue 3-inch-wide black crochet trim to neckline. Make a bow using 25 inches of trim, leaving ends long. Hot-glue bow to center of collar.

◀ metal detector

Neatly cut around a cool graphic from an old rock t-shirt. Hot-glue its edges evenly onto the center of a white tank top.

pom-pom squad ▲

Hot-glue sequin trim around neckline, then
add pom-pom trim below the sequins and along armholes.
Knot 2 minitassels around center pom-pom.

ribbon-front **halter**

Duplicate celebrity style with this fun top. Now, if we could figure out how to duplicate celebs' bank accounts too, we'd be set!

- plain black t-shirt
- 1 yard of 2-inch-wide pink satin ribbon
- 1 ½ yards of 1-inch-wide black elastic ribbon
- scissors
- ruler
- needle and thread

1. Cut off the top of the t-shirt under armpits so it's like a tube top, then turn it so the bottom hem is at the top.

2. Cut a 2-inch vertical slit in front, 1 inch in from left seam, and ½ inch down from the top. Make another 2-inch slit 1 inch to the right and parallel to the first slit.

3. Repeat Step 2 on the right side. You'll now have 2 "belt loops."

4. Repeat Steps 2 and 3 on back of top. Weave pink ribbon through all loops, tying ends in a knot in front.

5. Cut black ribbon in half. On inside of
top, stitch end of one ribbon above front left belt
loop. Repeat with other ribbon above right belt
loop to create two straps to tie behind your neck.

accessories

Just as pretty curtains or a bunch of throw pillows can make the style of a room, accessories can **transform an outfit.** The best part is that you don't have to spend more than the outfit you're wearing to **find just the right extra touch.** Especially not when you make it yourself!

In this chapter, see how to assemble a chunky beaded necklace on page 52 that will leave your friends **begging to know where you found it.** Need a fashion-forward, fun-to-look-at device for clocking the minutes until your most boring class is over? Try out the ribbon watch set on page 60. Blah shoes are always a style killer, but **don't blow all that babysitting money** on fancy footwear. If your ballet flats are a little tired-looking, or just look like everyone else's, **give them a makeover!** Check out decorated ballet flats on page 68 to see how. Sometimes the accessories you don't wear can make as **strong a statement** as the ones you do. Take your store-bought makeup bag. Looks just like the one most of your friends have, doesn't it? Well the polka-dot makeup bag on page 78 will change that! All of these projects are perfect for CG!s– simple, smart, and **loaded with style!**

bauble **heads**

Celebs may pay big bucks for vintage necklaces, but you can Make It Yourself and get the same look for much less.

lady lariat

Cut a 44-inch knotted, plastic bead necklace apart between 2 of the beads. Poke a 1-inch piece of wire through the hole on a colorful pendant; attach it to the necklace by twisting the wire between the bottom 2 beads on one end. Repeat on the other end with a second pendant.

queen bead

Lay a 20-inch strand of plain wooden beads on a newspaper in a well-ventilated area. Spray-paint the front of the beads with a can of silver-white spray paint. Let dry. Turn over and spray-paint the back of the beads. Let dry.

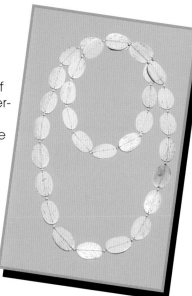

miss link

Use a pair of needle-nose pliers to pry open the last link on one end of a 2-foot, ½-inch-wide metal chain. Link it to the other end and use the pliers to close the ring. Open the jump ring on a pendant in the same metal tone as the chain, pass it through a link on the chain and close it.

jeweled **necklace**

Take a spool of thread and one of Grandma's old brooches and create a pendant that's all you.

easy

- • black sewing thread
- • 1 brooch
- • scissors
- • masking tape

1. Cut 9 pieces of thread, each 27 inches long. Knot them all together at one end.

2. Separate the threads into 3 sets, each with 3 strands. Braid the sets tightly together. (Tip: Pin the knotted end to a small cushion or the arm of an upholstered chair before you braid.)

3. Knot the other end of the braid.

4. Tie the middle of the braid around the center of the pin in back of the brooch.

5. If the brooch wobbles on the string, or turns sideways, anchor it to the braid with tape.

6. Tie the necklace around your neck. Voilà!

chunky beaded
necklace

Got half an hour? Make yourself a hip new necklace! If you like this one, try using all one color or a pattern of different colors rather than black and white.

- **2 yards of heavy-duty elastic thread**
- **32 medium-size (10mm) black beads**
- **12 medium-size (10mm) white beads**
- **needle with large-eye**
- **scissors**

1. Thread the needle with the elastic thread. Pull the thread through and bring the two ends together so that you have a double length of thread.

2. Securely double-knot the ends together—make the knot bigger than the hole in your beads (you'll cut if off later so don't worry if it's clunky).

3. Thread beads one at a time over the needle and slide them onto the elastic; use the pattern that we made at right, or create a pattern of your own.

4. When all the beads are on, carefully and securely double-knot the elastic ends together close to the beads. Cut off the excess elastic (remove the needle), and you're done! Wear the double knot at the back of your neck so it doesn't show.

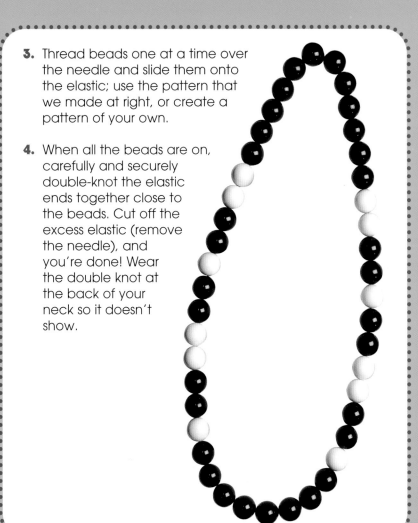

key **necklace**

These easy-to-make jewels are one of a kind and totally cutting edge. Hmm. . . sort of reminds us of you!

easy

- **1 uncut household key**
- **1 package small rhinestones**
- **delicate chain necklace**
- **craft glue**
- **tweezers**

1. Neatly coat one whole side of the key with a thin layer of craft glue. Use the tweezers to place rhinestones all over the key, covering it completely or letting some of the metal show through.

2. Let key dry 2 hours.

3. Thread the chain through the hole in the top of the key and fasten it around your neck. For different looks, swap the chain for a piece of thin ribbon or suede or satin cord.

monogrammed
velvet **bangles**

These bracelets are such fun to create, you'll be
making them for all your friends.

medium

- **1 yard of velvet ribbon**
- **1 plastic bangle**
- **1 package small rhinestones**
- **hot-glue gun and glue sticks**
- **scissors**
- **tweezers**

1. Hot-glue one end of the velvet ribbon to the inside
   of the bangle. Wind the ribbon around the bangle,
   overlapping it a bit each time to completely cover the
   plastic. End on the inside of the bangle and cut off
   excess ribbon. Glue the end to the inside of the bangle.

2. Grab a rhinestone with the tweezers, put a dab of hot glue on the back, and stick it onto bracelet. Continue to create a fun pattern or spell out your friend's initials like we did on ours. Let dry 2 hours.

beaded **bracelet**

Make this bracelet to wear out tonight. Just be sure to leave enough time for the glue to dry! The beads make plain thread spools bauble-icious!

- 1 empty thread spool
- craft glue
- 1 package each 1.5-mm seed beads and 5-mm beads
- ball-link chain bracelet
- tweezers

1. Neatly coat the main body of the spool with a thin layer of glue. Sprinkle seed beads all over to cover. Let dry 2 hours.

2. Coat the rounded molding at each end of the spool with glue. Use the tweezers to place the beads around the edges. Let dry 2 hours.

3. Thread the chain bracelet through the spool. Fasten around your wrist. Make 2 bracelets in different colors and wear them together!

ribbon **watch set**

The hardest thing about this great gift is tying the watch on at the end!

- 1 inexpensive watch (maybe an old one you don't wear)
- ²/₃ yard each of 4 different-colored ¹/₂-inch-wide grosgrain, velvet, or satin ribbons
- gift box (optional)
- scissors

1. Detach the watch from the band. Most watches have a spring bar—push the ends together like a toilet paper holder and the band should pop off. If not, carefully cut the band away from the watch.

2. Cut each ribbon into a 20-inch-long piece, cutting the ends on diagonals. Thread one ribbon through the bars and under the back of the watch to form a new band. Put it in a box with the three other ribbon bands to make a set. Offer to help your friend tie it on—it's tricky, but oh-so cute!

61

button **brooch**

We picked bright, colorful buttons for summer, but pick whichever ones (in different sizes, colors, and shapes) show off your personal style!

- **cardboard (try a cereal box)**
- **craft glue**
- **assorted buttons**
- **pin backing**
- **scissors**

1. On cardboard, sketch a shape you like for the base of the brooch (ours is a 2-inch-high triangle).

2. Neatly cut out the shape.

3. Coat one side of the cardboard cutout with a thin layer of glue. Arrange the larger buttons all over the shape in a random pattern; press them into the glue to adhere.

4. Arrange several smaller buttons on top, overlapping the bottom layer; lift one at a time and then glue on. Let dry 2 hours.

5. Turn brooch over and glue pin backing to center. Let dry 2 hours. Pin to a tank or even your beach bag!

ballerina **slippers**

Turn shoes you never wear into a new pair with satin ribbon and some nail polish.

- **3 yards of $3/_{16}$-inch-wide satin ribbon**
- **1 pair of flats or slides**
- **scissors**
- **fabric glue**
- **nail polish**

1. Cut the ribbon in half.

2. Mark the center of the back of each shoe (on the inside) as a guide for attaching the ribbon—the mark should be just above the heel but not so high that the glued-on ribbon would dig into your ankle.

3. Fold each piece of ribbon in half to find the middle, then saturate that part with fabric glue, and adhere it to the mark inside each shoe. Let it dry overnight.

4. Use bright nail polish to paint a design on each shoe.

5. Crisscross the ribbons up around your ankles and tie in a bow. Cut off any excess. Then walk the walk, girl!

decorated
ballet flats

Give those basic shoes in the back of your closet some CPR—and bring them back to life!

- **1 pair of plain flats**
- **several small decorative trinkets like pins, charms, or puffy fabric stickers**
- **craft glue**
- **paper towels**

1. Clean surface of the shoes with a damp paper towel. Wipe dry.

2. If you're using pins or charms, carefully remove the pin backs or the charm hooks so they won't get in the way when you glue.

3. Decide where you want to position the items—we placed ours off center on the top of the shoes. Then carefully glue them in place using craft cement.

4. Let dry 3 hours before wearing.

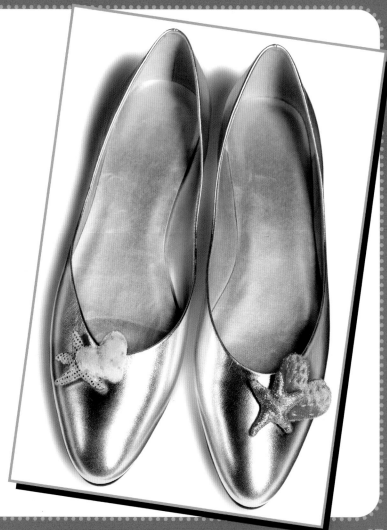

grab **bag**

Follow these simple steps to stitch some fancy fabric into an absolutely scrumptious new bag!

- **½ yard of heavy woven fabric**
- **scissors**
- **needle and thread**

1. Cut a 20" by 14" rectangle from the fabric.

2. Fold under and then sew a ½-inch hem on each 14" edge. These will be the top of the bag.

3. Lay the fabric flat and draw a 6" by 1 ½" oblong handle opening, centered 1" from one of the hemmed edges. Repeat at the other hemmed edge. Cut out the openings. If you like, sew around each opening to keep it from raveling.

4. Fold the fabric in half, with the wrong side out, so the hemmed 14" edges meet.

5. Sew the layers together along each short edge (from the fold to the hemmed top edge). Turn the bag right side out and go!

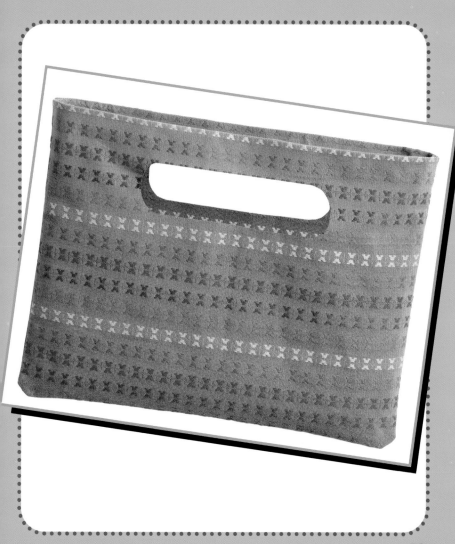

ring handle **bag**

**Take a trip to the fabric or craft store. And then?
Baby's got a brand new bag!**

- **¹/₂ yard of cotton twill fabric**
- **two 6-inch-diameter circular handbag handles**
- **scissors**
- **straight pins**
- **needle and thread**

1. Cut two 16-by-18-inch rectangles from the fabric. Lay them on top of each other with the right sides facing in. Sew together on one 16-inch edge to form the bottom of the bag. Then sew together on each 18-inch edge, stopping 5 inches from the top on each.

2. Lay one handle at the top of one side of the bag and fold a 2-inch hem down through the ring. Pin it in a few places—be careful not to pin through to the second side of the bag. Sew the hem to encase the handle. Go slowly—the fabric will start to gather as you sew. Turn the bag over and repeat on the other side with the second handle.

3. Turn the whole bag right side out. Now fill it up with all your stuff and go!

slouchy ribbon **bag**

This bag is a carbon copy of one celebrities love. It is said that imitation is the highest form of flattery. Think the stars will be happy?

- **2 yards of black cotton fabric**
- **2 yards 1¹/₂-inch-wide pink satin ribbon**
- **scissors**
- **needle and black thread**

1. Cut two 30-by-13-inch pieces of fabric. Lay them on top of each other with the right sides facing in. Stitch together along both 13-inch edges.

2. Loosely sew ¹/₂-inch stitches across one 30-inch edge of one fabric piece. Pull thread tight to gather; knot. Repeat on corresponding edge of facing fabric. Create the bottom of the bag by stitching together the opposite 30-inch edges.

3. Form a "waistband" on top of bag: Cut a 28-by-4-inch strip of fabric. Sew short ends together to make a ring. Stitch ¹/₂-inch hem on one edge. Slip the ring inside the

open edge of the bag—be sure the right sides of the fabric are together—and line up the cut (unhemmed) edges. Pin and sew together.

4. Fold the waistband in half along the top of the bag and sew the hemmed edge to the bag.

5. Turn bag right side out. Cut two 3-by-$\frac{1}{4}$-inch strips of fabric. Stitch to front of the bag as belt loops. Cut a 1-by-24-inch strip. Sew ends inside top of bag to form strap.

6. Thread ribbon though belt loops and tie in a bow.

Note: Since this project is a lot of sewing, you may want to use a sewing machine if you're ready for it!

customized **tote bag**

Tote your stuff in a bag that's as unique as you are.

- $1/_2$ yard each of two colors satin fabric
- 2 yards each of 10 different ribbons, lace, or sequined trim
- scissors
- needle and thread

1. Cut one 14-by-24-inch piece from each fabric. Lay the pieces on top of each other, shiny sides facing in. Sew together on all edges, leaving a 4-inch opening. Turn right side out through opening; then stitch it closed.

2. Fold fabric in half so 14-inch sides meet (with the color you ultimately want on the outside facing in). Sew together along each short edge (from the fold to the open edge). Turn right side out.

3. To make the first handle, cut and then knot ten 30-inch-long strands of different ribbons together at one end. Braid them together and knot at other end. To make the second handle, braid the 10 remaining 42-inch-long strands of ribbon, tying off with a large knot 12 inches before the end, so you have loose ribbons hanging.

4. On one side of the bag, stitch ends of first handle to the inside, 1 inch from top and 2 inches in from each seam. On opposite side of bag, cut a 2-inch vertical slit through both fabrics, 1 inch down and 2 inches in from one side seam. Pull the braided end of the second handle through the slit to the inside of bag and sew it 2 inches from the opposite seam. Pull knot against slit.

painted
straw bag

Try this quick change for a summer bag that is perfect for carrying your stuff to the beach.

- 1 plain straw bag
- 1 can of hot-pink spray paint
- assorted colored sequins
- newspaper
- craft glue

1. Spread out newspaper on a work surface (or better yet, your driveway or some other place where there's lots of fresh air) and put the bag on top. Stuff some newspaper into the bag to protect the inside lining from spray paint.

2. Spray-paint the entire outside of bag, including the handles. Let dry three hours. You can give it another coat of paint if it needs it.

3. Using tiny dabs of craft glue, carefully apply as many sequins as you like randomly all over the bag.

4. Let dry another two hours to make sure all of the sequins are secure.

polka-dot
makeup bag

Fill this cute bag with some Make-It-Yourself beauty products—try the Lip Gloss Trio on page 94.

* **1 plastic tablecloth in a fun pattern (we used polka dots) or $1/2$ yard flannel-backed plastic cloth**
* **2 safety pins**
* **3 Velcro tabs**
* **1 yard of 1-inch-wide striped ribbon in a pattern or color that contrasts with tablecloth**
* **needle and thread**
* **scissors**
* **hot-glue gun and glue sticks**

1. Cut a 12-by-15-inch rectangle from the tablecloth.

2. Fold under and then sew a $1/2$-inch hem on each 12-inch edge. These will be the top of the bag.

3. Fold fabric in half, with patterned side in, so the hemmed 12-inch edges meet.

4. Sew the layers together along each short edge (from the fold to the hemmed top edge).

5. To create rounded corners, put a safety pin through each bottom corner, 1 inch in from the point. Turn the bag right side out.

6. Separate the halves of the Velcro tabs. Space the stiff halves equally along one hemmed edge on the inside of bag; hot-glue in place. Glue the soft halves onto the other hem, opposite the stiff ones.

7. Wrap ribbon around bag. Tie a bow as shown in the photo. Hot-glue ribbon in place on the back of bag at the top, then untie the bow and glue the ribbon down the back and up the front, stopping 3 inches from top.

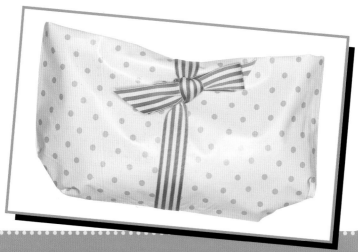

beauty

For most of us, **beauty products are as essential as food.** But sometimes the money we spend to stock up on them means we may not be able to afford to eat! Then **take all those pricey products** we like to give our friends, moms, sisters, grandmothers… *Caa-ching!* Good news: **You can have all the potions** you need to look radiant—and still have money left over to **splurge at the food court!**

If your locks are lacking luster, try the all-natural avocado mask for dry hair on page 82 and restore the shine! **Rejuvenate yourself** with our tub-time essentials—from fizzy bath bombs on page 90 to winter bath soak shakers on page 92. And about those **beauty gifts you just gotta give . . .** Try the surprise soaps on page 86 or the cocoa butter bonbons on page 98—sure to please all the **chocolate lovers in your life.** Remember, with a little creativity and a little time, **you can make something** unforgettable!

avocado mask for dry hair

To make this protein-rich mask, we recommend using organic ingredients. They're better for the environment, but they're usually more expensive.

- 1 ripe avocado, pitted and mashed
- 2 tablespoons plain yogurt
- 1 egg
- 1 tablespoon jojoba oil
- $\frac{1}{2}$ teaspoon rosemary oil

1. In a blender, combine avocado, yogurt, egg, jojoba oil, and rosemary oil on a medium setting until smooth.

2. Massage the mixture into your scalp and work through clean, dry hair from roots to tips. Leave on for 20 minutes, then rinse and shampoo as usual.

leave-in
conditioner

Fabric softener can do more than make your undies soft; it can detangle your hair!

- ½ cup liquid fabric softener
- 1 cup water
- spray bottle

1. Pour fabric softener and water into the spray bottle. Shake well.

2. Spritz five times over clean, damp hair; comb through, then style.

Warning: The fragrance in fabric softener might irritate sensitive skin, so do a patch test first. Spritz the mixture on your forearm and wait 24 hours. If there's no redness, you're good to go!

surprise **soaps**

These cleansing bars have a surprise for the lucky girl who gets them as a gift! This recipe makes three large bars of special soaps.

- **4-5 bars of colored glycerine soap**
- **several small gift items that can get wet (like plastic toys, key chains, or mini nail polishes)**
- **washcloth and ribbon (optional)**
- **cooking oil (vegetable)**
- **3 small containers for soap molds (try muffin-pan cups)**

1. Using a sharp knife and cutting board, chop up soap into small chunks . Put in the chunks into microwave-safe glass bowl.

2. Microwave soap for 1 minute on high (or repeat at 30-second intervals, stirring in between) until soap melts into a liquid.

3. While the soap is melting, grease the molds with a little oil.

4. Place one or two of the small gifts flat in the center of each mold.

5. Pour the melted soap into the molds, completely covering the gifts.

6. Place molds in refrigerator for about 20 minutes or so.

7. When soaps are cool and firm to the touch, turn molds over and gently press to release soaps.

8. Let soaps sit overnight to harden.

9. For a gift, wrap soaps in a new, bright washcloth and tie with ribbon, if desired.

peppermint
bath salts

The smell of peppermint is perfect for a holiday gift! This recipe makes one 20-ounce jar.

- **2 cups Epsom salts**
- **½ cup rock salt or sea salt**
- **peppermint essential oil**
- **water-based red food coloring**
- **one 20-ounce glass jar**
- **peppermint candies or candy canes and red ribbon**

1. Place 1 cup Epsom salts and ¼ cup rock salt in a medium-size bowl.

2. Add 2-3 drops peppermint oil; stir well to evenly distribute. Set aside.

3. Place the remaining Epsom salts and rock salt in a separate medium-size bowl.

4. Add 2-3 drops red food coloring to the second bowl. Mix well until the color is a nice, even shade.

5. Now add 2-3 drops peppermint oil to the red mixture; stir well to evenly distribute.

6. Pour the white salts and red salts into the jar in alternating layers to create a striped candy cane effect.

7. Place lid on top. If your jar lid can be filled, place some candies in it the way we did. Or glue peppermint candies on the lid or tie on a candy cane with a large red ribbon.

fizzy bath bombs

Drop a bomb in the bath to make it frothy, colorful, and fragrant! These instructions are for one bath bomb but since everyone will want one, stock up on extra supplies!

hard

- 1 1/2 cups baking soda
- 1/2 teaspoon water-based food coloring
- 1/2 teaspoon fragrance oil of your choice
- 3/4 cup citric acid
- water, in a spray bottle
- 1 ball-shape soap or candy mold (2 1/2-inch diameter)
- cellophane giftwrap
- 1 yard colorful narrow ribbon
- scissors

1. Mix together baking soda, food coloring, and fragrance oil in a medium-size glass bowl to evenly distribute color and scent. Add citric acid. Blend with your hands until mixture begins to hold its shape when pressed together (like wet sand). If the mixture needs more moisture, mist it with water.

2. Pack mixture tightly into each half of the mold. Level off molds and wipe away any excess. Gently press out each half onto a waxed paper-lined cookie sheet. Set in refrigerator overnight.

3. The next day, remove bath bombs from fridge. Gently place two halves together to form a sphere. Wrap in cellophane and tie ends with ribbon.

winter bath
soak shakers

Make tub time even more relaxing with these three different scents!

easy

- three 3-inch tall spice canisters, empty, clean, and dry
- white Contact paper
- white adhesive labels
- $\frac{1}{2}$ yard each of $\frac{1}{4}$-inch-wide colorful grosgrain ribbon
- 3 cups powdered milk
- $1\frac{1}{2}$ cups Epsom salts
- 5 drops each of orange, cinnamon, and peppermint essential oils
- 3 zip-tight plastic bags
- markers, black and colors to match ribbons
- scissors
- hot-glue gun and glue sticks

1. Wrap canisters in Contact paper to cover old labels. With the markers, draw borders and write contents on the adhesive labels; cut to fit front of the canisters. Stick on. Wrap a ribbon around each of the canisters and tie in a bow; adhere ribbon with hot-glue if it slides off.

2. Place 1 cup powdered milk and ½ cup Epsom salts in a zip-tight plastic bag. Add orange essential oil. Shake well to mix. Repeat process in separate bags using the cinnamon and peppermint essential oils.

3. Pour each mixture into its own canister and close tightly. Shake, shake, shake into your bath!

lip gloss trio

Carry this around in our Polka-Dot Makeup Bag (page 78) or one of the many totes from the Accessories section!

- **3 small plastic containers with lids (try bead sorter boxes)**
- **3 teaspoons grated beeswax**
- **3 teaspoons petroleum jelly**
- **1/2 teaspoon each of 3 different colored lipsticks (use remnant bits or inexpensive ones)**
- **hot-glue gun and glue sticks**
- **empty soup can, clean and dry**

1. Hot-glue containers together to make a one-piece holder for your trio.

2. Place 1 teaspoon beeswax, 1 teaspoon petroleum jelly, and 1 color of the lipstick in the soup can.

3. Fill a small pot with 3 inches of water. Bring to boiling. Reduce heat to low. Using oven mitt, place can in pot. Melt mixture, stirring frequently until blended. Carefully pour into one of the containers.

4. Clean out the can and repeat two times using other lipstick colors. Refrigerate until solid. Make different combinations of gloss shades to fit each of your friends' favorite colors for gifts.

eggnog
body lotion

**Who the heck wants a partridge in a pear tree?!
No one! So skip the traditional stuff and make
your friend a gift that's as one-of-a-kind as she is!**

medium

- **2 egg yolks**
- **1/2 cup heavy cream or
  half-and-half**
- **1 tablespoon witch hazel**
- **1/2 teaspoon vanilla extract**
- **1/4 cup canola or almond oil**
- **1 glass bottle with cap, at least 8
  ounces, clean and dry**
- **1/2 yard 1/4-inch-wide colorful
  sheer ribbon (optional)**

1. In a blender, combine the egg yolks, heavy cream,
   witch hazel, and vanilla extract on a medium setting
   until well mixed.

2. Switch to the lowest setting, and with the blender still
   running, add the oil a little bit at a time (through the
   hole in the top of the cover) until it is fully mixed in and
   the mixture has a creamy consistency.

3. Pour the finished lotion into the bottle; seal the bottle.

4. Decorate the bottle with ribbon, if desired.

Note: *Make sure your friend knows that since it contains no preservatives, this lotion should be used within two weeks—and it must be stored in the refrigerator!*

cocoa butter
bonbons

It's like having a spa at home when you make this recipe for moisturizing bonbons. *Ooo la la!*

medium

- $\frac{1}{2}$ cup cocoa butter
- 1 tablespoon coconut oil
- $\frac{1}{8}$ teaspoon vitamin E oil
- $\frac{1}{2}$ teaspoon chocolate fragrance oil
- candy mold with cups of any shape (this makes eight $2\frac{1}{2}$-inch bonbons)
- 8 foil candy wrappers

1. Heat cocoa butter in small saucepan over very low heat until melted (about 30 seconds). Add coconut oil; remove from heat.

2. Add remaining oils and stir well.

3. Pour mixture into molds. Place in freezer for an hour to set. Remove and carefully pop out each bonbon. Place each one in a foil candy wrapper.

4. Arrange bonbons in an empty candy box with the instructions written on a pretty note card: "Hold a bonbon in your hand to warm it up, then smooth it on your body!"

healing
hand scrub

This is quick and so easy—it can be whipped up right in your own kitchen! The salt in this scrub exfoliates, and the oils nourish and moisturize dry skin.

- ½ cup sea salt
- ½ cup olive oil
- 2 tablespoons coconut oil
- 1 tablespoons rosemary oil

1. Mix all the ingredients together, then massage the scrub onto your hands for about a minute.

2. Rinse with warm water and pat dry.

3. For a finishing touch, don't forget a manicure with polish that suits your personality!

honey & almond
body scrub

The almonds help exfoliate your skin in this sweet spa treatment.

easy

- ¹/₂ cup honey
- 1 cup finely ground almonds
- 2 ¹/₂ tablespoons lemon juice

1. Use a food processor to grind the almonds. (If you don't have a food processor, place the almonds in a plastic sandwich bag and use a wooden mallet to crush them.)

2. Blend the ground almonds, honey, and lemon juice in a bowl.

3. After you wash your body in the shower, use your hands to massage the scrub all over your legs, arms, stomach, back, and chest, avoiding the delicate skin on your face. Spend extra time rubbing the scrub onto rough spots like your elbows, heels, and knees.

4. Rinse with warm water.

solid perfume

Choose your favorite essential oil to make your very own fragrance.

- small 10-ounce jar with lid
- $1/4$ yard of $1/2$-inch-wide ribbon
- assorted rhinestones or sequins
- craft glue
- 3 teaspoons grated beeswax
- $1/2$ cup petroleum jelly
- $1/4$ ounce essential oil of your choice
- empty soup can, clean and dry

1. Glue ribbon around jar. Glue rhinestones to ribbon in any design you like.

2. Place beeswax and petroleum jelly in the soup can.

3. Fill a small pot with 3 inches of water. Bring to boiling. Reduce heat to low. Using oven mitt, place can in pot. Melt mixture, stirring frequently until blended. Remove from heat. Mix in oil.

4. Pour into decorated jar. Refrigerate with lid off until it's solid; then seal with the lid.

chocolate mint
cookie **foot scrub**

**This minty foot treatment is the perfect gift for a
friend, even if she doesn't have stinky feet!**

easy

- **1 cup turbinado sugar**
- **$1/4$ cup rolled oats**
- **1 tablespoon cocoa powder**
- **$1/2$ cup pure almond oil**
- **5 drops of peppermint
  essential oil**
- **1 30-ounce glass jar with a seal-
  tight lid, clean and dry**
- **wooden spoon to fit jar**
- **1 yard of 2-inch-wide
  grosgrain ribbon**
- **white adhesive labels**
- **assorted green markers**

1. Mix sugar, oats, and cocoa powder in a glass bowl. Stir
   in almond oil a little at a time until all dry ingredients are
   moistened. Stir in peppermint oil. Transfer to jar.

2. Seal jar. Decorate label with markers. Tie ribbon on jar.
   Slip spoon for scooping into hinge on jar.

chocolate mint cookie
FOOT SCRUB

index

photo credits

boys-of-the-week panties jewele
anks for everything! tie-dyed m
chain t-shirt sequined tank top
ank and skirt ribbon-front halte
necklace key necklace beaded
ballet flats painted straw bag m
bag ring handle bag slouchy rib
bag avocado mask for dry hair
almond body scrub winter bath
peppermint bath salts eggnog
izzy bath bombs lip gloss trio s
ace t-shirt studded stunner spe
sweat scarf, top, and jeans cut
ank top ruched tube dress pat
heads jeweled necklace chunky
ibbon watch set button brooch
grammed velvet bangles balleri
bag customized tote bag polka-
n conditioner healing hands sc
hakers chocolate mint cookie
otion cocoa butter bonbons su